Your

I wanted to show my appreciation that you support my work so I've put together a free gift for you.

Slowcooker Essentials Cookbook
http://thezenfactory.com/smoke_like_pro_book/

Just visit the link above to download it now.

I know you will love this gift.

Thanks!

Table Of Content

Table Of Content 2

Introduction 6

Meats 7

    Meats Grades 9

    How To Select The Best Cut 14

The Smoker 16

    The best cheap and expensive smokers 19

    Homemade Smoker 24

Wood Types and Uses 26

Pit and Fire Management 28

Trimming Meats: The Best Cuts to Smoke 31

The Cooking: Tips and Tricks 34

Serving and Eating 39

    The Best Sauces and Side Dishes to Serve with Smoked Meat 41

The Top 25 Smoked Meat, Sauces, Rubs Recipes 45

Chili Sweet Rub 45

    Ingredients: 45

    Directions: 46

Multi-purpose Rub 47

    Ingredients: 47

    Directions: 47

Basic Rub 48

    Ingredients: 48

    Directions: 48

Honey Sauce 49

    Ingredients: 49

Directions: 50

Spicy Black Sauce 51

Ingredients: 51

Directions: 51

Garlicky Mashed Potato 52

Ingredients: 52

Directions: 52

Smoked Salmon Spread 54

Ingredients: 54

Directions: 54

Spicy Coleslaw Salad 55

Ingredients: 55

Directions: 55

Summer Salad 57

Ingredients: 57

Directions: 57

Cheese Sticks 58

Ingredients: 58

Directions: 58

Smoked Corn on the Cob 59

Ingredients: 59

Directions: 59

Cheesy Smoked Pork's Shepherd Pie 61

Ingredients: 61

Directions: 61

Coleslaw Barbecue 62

Ingredients: 62

Directions: 62

Smoked Fajitas 63

    Ingredients: 63

    Directions: 63

Smokey Apple Pie 65

    Ingredients: 65

    Directions: 65

Perfectly Smoked Cornish Game Hens..............................67

    Ingredients: 67

    Directions: 67

Rubbed and Smoked Chicken 68

    Ingredients: 68

    Rub: 68

    Directions: 68

Smoked Quarters 69

    Ingredients: 69

    Rub: 69

    Directions: 69

Smoked Turkey 71

    Ingredients: 71

    Rub: 71

    Directions: 71

Basic Quarters 72

    Ingredients: 72

    Marinade: 72

    Directions: 72

Semi Sweet Smoked Salmon 74

    Ingredients: 74

    Marinade: 74

Directions: 74

Brisket pan 76

Ingredients: 76

Rub: 76

Directions: 76

Apple Ribs 78

Ingredients: 78

Rub: 78

Directions: 78

Smoky Pork Butt 80

Ingredients: 80

Rub: 80

Directions: 80

Dripping Ribs 82

Ingredients: 82

Rub: 82

Directions: 82

Conclusion 85

Introduction

I want to thank you and congratulate you for downloading the book, "Smoke It Like a Pro: The Best Smoking Meat Guide & 25 Master Recipes From A Competition Barbecue Team

This book contains proven steps and strategies on how to smoke meat starting with an explicit chapter about the grades of meat, the types of smokers and the characteristics of each one, how to build a smoker in your house, how to smoke different types of meats and keep them moist and juicy, how to trim the cuts of meat before smoking them as well as other tips and techniques that will help you master the art and basics of smoking.

You don't have to be an expert or chef to read this book, if you love smoking meat and or simply want to learn how to do it; I welcome you join me in the depths of this amazing and explicit book.

You might not know anything about smoking or know little, but one you finish this book, you will get people asking for tips from you and fighting to get a piece of your smoked meat. Food has always been and will always stay and amazing way to gather families and friends as well as bring the smile and joy to the face of people.

Thanks again for downloading this book, I hope you enjoy it!

Meats

« Meat» when I think of this word I immediately starts imagining smoked meat covered with sauce and ready to be ravished, I don't know about you but meat is the food number 1 in my life; it is one of the reasons that I'm alive till now.

You can cook the meat in so many different and various ways, however before you does it, you need to know how to choose the perfect cut of meat. Many people says that they don't like meat because it is simply not tasty and full of fats, have you ever stopped for a second and thought that maybe it is your fault that the meat your eating is not tasty? Maybe you didn't choose the right cut or maybe you just didn't cook it well?

Nobody is perfect; every single person on earth makes mistakes, but instead of abandoning meats and hating it or simply giving up on trying to make it better; you can make your life much more interesting and dive in its sea to discover its hidden secrets and its true marvelous taste.

Choosing the right cut of meat doesn't require you to be a scientist or a butcher, all you need is to read and memorize some few information on how to pick the right cut starting by getting yourself familiar with the grades of meat and the best way to get the best cut from each grade whether it is Beef, Veal, Lamb or Pork.

Grading is based on the nationally uniform Federal standards of quality where the grade the meat according to its yielding, juiciness, and tenderness...Each grading of type of meat is different from the other, for example: Beef meat is graded into 3 parts whereas Veal/Calf is graded into 5 parts and you get to make the final choice of what you want.

Meats Grades

Beef Grades:

The grades of Beef Quality is sectioned into 3 parts, each of them has specific characteristics that makes it special and differ it for the other parts. These grades are:

1. Prime Grade:

This grade is the most expensive one and it is usually served in hotels and restaurants as well as expensive places because it is derived from young and well fed male cattle. This cut is so juicy and tender which makes it perfect for any type of cooking whether you want to grill it, roast it...

Tips and tricks: This lean cut doesn't need too much cooking or flavors, a pinch of salt and pepper will take you to the moon and back.

2. The Choice Grade:

This cut is also known for its high quality but it is less then the prime grade not to mention that it is also less marbled. You can always go for steaks and roasts from the round, loin and rib because they tend to be more juicy and tender.

Tips and Tricks: To help this cut keeps its juices and prevent it from drying, cook it or sear it with some butter; it will keep it moist and juicy.

3. The Select Grade:

This grade is the cheapest and has less marbling as well as flavor and juices than the other grades not to mention that it is somewhat dry but the rib and loin are always little bit more tender then the other parts.

Tips and Tricks: The best way to keep this cut moist and tender is by coating It with some sauce like Worcestershire sauce and rest it for at least 30 min before cooking it.

Calf/Veal Grades:

Veal is a tender meat that comes from young calf with 16 to 18 weeks. Veal meat grading is different from beef as it is sectioned to 5 grades.

1. The Prime Grade:

This grade is the best and most expensive one because it is the tender, juicy and marvelously marbled which makes it perfect for any type of cooking.

Tips and Tricks: Just like the prime grade in beef, this grade doesn't require much work to flavor it because it is already. A pinch of salt and black pepper will bring the best of it.

2. The Choice Grade:

This grade is also known to be a high quality like the prime grade but it tends to be a little bit dry not to mention that it also has less marbling then the prime grade. The best and most tender cuts in this grade are the shoulders, roast and chops.

Tips and Tricks:

To make these slightly dry and less tender cuts like breast, shank and neck moist and juicy, braise them before cooking them.

3. The Good, The Utility and The Cull grade:

These grades are not common and you won't usually find them in stores but they always tend to be less tender and juicy then the prime and the choice grade.

Lamb Grades:

Just like Calf meat, lamb also is sectioned into several grading but the only grades that you can find in stores are the prime and choice grades. Lamb meat is derived from lambs less then 1 year old because they tend to be much more tender and juicier not to mention that it is so easy to cook. It is highly recommended to buy graded lamb USDA because if it is not, you might be stuck with low quality meat.

1. Prime Grade:

As it is known, the prime choice is the best grade at all, because it is so juicy and tender. It basically has the qualities of great meat.

Tips and Tricks:

The prime choice of any type of meat doesn't need any tips or tricks to get the best out of it because it is simply good as it is.

2. The Choice Grade:

This grade of lamb meat also comes with a high quality although it is less marbled then the prime grade but it still makes a great meal. The shoulder cuts, leg and roasts are the most tender and juicier parts.

Tips and Tricks:

The best way to prevent any type of meat from drying is by braising them. Although this grade of meat is juicy and tender it is better to be safe then sorry.

Pork Grades:

Unlike lamb, Beef and Calf; pork is not graded because it simply doesn't need to. It is derived from specific animals that were fed and raised to have tender and juicy meat that is compatible with all types of cooking. You can grill, roast, fry, or cook it in a slow cooker, if you cooked it right it will stay juicy, moist and tender.

Tips and Tricks:

To get the best cuts, try to get cuts with the lowest amounts of fat. Slow cooking is also the best way to cook pork if you want it to be juicy, tender and melts in the mouth.

Since pork has lot of fat, it is recommended to eat it with fresh salad so balance it.

How To Select The Best Cut

You might be one of the people who think that choosing the right cut of meat is the hardest thing ever and often leave that decision for the butcher. What you don't know, is that you can actually choose the best cut for a nice price easily without needing anyone's help except for your butcher sometimes.

You can't always rely on the butcher to decide for you and choose for you a nice cut, it is time to take you matters in your own hands and make your own decisions by learning the basics of choosing the right meat.

1. Befriend the butcher:

Nice cuts of meat can definitely be expensive, but what you don't know is that the butcher knows many different cuts that will make a great bargain for cheap price. When you befriend your butcher, you will always get know the cheap cuts with a good quality that will make your meals tastier.

2. With bone or without?

The hardest decision is whether to choose a steak with a bone or without it?

You don't have to think about it twice anymore, bone it is. When you choose a steak or cut of meat with bone you will get it for a cheaper price and you'll get to benefit from it in more then one way. If you don't like your meat with a bone you can always take it out and use it later to a beef, pork or lamb broth, not mention that it will make it much more easier for the butcher to prepare it for you, which is a great start for your friendship.

3. Why ignore fat?

Since we were children, we used to be told by our parents that fats are not healthy so we try to ignore it as much possible and choose the leanest cuts with the smallest amount of fat. I totally agree with that but a meat without fat is nothing at all, because the fat you're trying all your life to ignore is the key to flavor your meat as well as the main ingredient that will keep it moist and juicy.

4. Know your meat by its color and shape:

The top 2 indictors of the freshness of any meat are unfortunately what many people ignore. Before you decide to buy any cut of meat, check it color first. The beef should be dark red not brown, the pork, chicken and lamb should be rosy.

After finding the nice color you're looking for, press on the cut of meat to test its firmness. If you found it so soft, it a cue that is a bad quality. The meat you're looking for should be firm and slightly soft.

Now that you know the basics of choosing the right cut of meat, all you need to do is to choose a nice recipe and prepare your meal as a chef. It will only take one bite to bring you back to reality and show you how much you have been missing your whole life.

If you are interested in my meat recipes, I have several other cookbooks that will blow your mind and teach you the art of cooking meat from scratch.

The Smoker

A smoker is a specific appliance used to cook some meals on a low temperature for a long period of time up to 15 h non-stop. Smoker is used outdoor because it uses smoke to cook the meals and derives it from burning woods, charcoal, pellets, gas or electricity. It is used to smoke almost all kinds of foods, from meat to poultry, veggies, fish and fruits.

The idea of smoking food originally came from our ancestor's caveman's life style as they used to hang the meat in their small caves which allows it to absorb the smoke whenever they illuminated fire in the cave.

Throughout the years and thanks to the development that humanity have known on so many levels, smoking seized from being a method to preserve foods and make them last longer to become a new method of cooking that enhances the flavor of the food, not to mention that it also adds to it its own flavor to give it a whole new amazing smoky meal.

There 3 common ways in smoking which are:

1. Cold Smoking:

Cold smoking is a method used to preserve foods for a long time without cooking them and it also enhances there flavor. The foods should be rubbed with some salt to keep the bacteria away then smoked on low temperature which starts from 68 F to 86 F.

2. Smoke Roasting:

This method refers to roasting or baking and smoking at the same time; which can be done in a smoke roaster, barbecue pit...In this case the temperature reaches up to 250 F.

3. Hot Smoking:

Hot smoking is the usual and most common method that requires smoking foods on high temperature up to 167 F or 225 F. It is simply about smoking food for a long time until it becomes thoroughly cooked, juicy and tender.

When it comes to smokers, there are 4 types of them that come with different characteristics and benefits as well as flavors. The available types of smokers are:

1. Electric Smoker:

This type of smokers are known for there amazing results because they are so easy to use and doesn't need you to keep checking on them all the time and fuel them. Once you adjust the setting to your liking, you can just go ahead and proceed with you daily routine leaving it to do what it does best "smoking".

The electric smokers are also known for their ability to hold more food then the other types of smokers; which makes them perfect for you if you want to smoke large quantities of food, the thing that makes it the most expensive one.

2. Charcoal Smokers:

Every Barbeque lover consider the charcoal smokers are the best when it comes to smoking food because they add an amazing and irresistible flavor to it and makes it much more delicious.

The best thing about it is that they have smokers that have a small compartment for water to keep you food tender and juicy. However, this type of smokers can be quite tough and frustrating to use because it requires lot of work beginning by lighting up the charcoal that might take up to 30 min.

In addition to that, this smoker can be quite expensive because it requires lot of charcoal which is not cheap at all, not to mention that it needs your constant attention to add more charcoal from time to time as well as prevent it from getting too hot and burning your food.

3. Propane Smokers:

Just like electric smokers, this type is also common and many people prefer it because you can simply adjust its setting and let it do all the work for you without having to keep checking it all the time.

The best feature of this smoker is its flexibility because you get to use it whenever and wherever you want; outside, indoor or you can take it with you on your camping trip without having to worry about anything.

4. Wood Pellet Smokers:

Wood pellets smokers are known to be expensive but their results are always remarkable. It is just like the propane and electric smoker, you don't have to babysit it to make sure it won't burn your food or not cook it at all because the auger system in it controls the pellets and add few by few whenever it needs to be added; it basically does all the work for you.

The amazing thing about it also is it that you don't get just the flavor of smoke in your food like it is for the electric and propane smokers, the wood pellets you use adds their own flavor and aroma as well which makes your food flavored and mouthwateri

The best cheap and expensive smokers

There are hundreds of smokers with different costs that you can choose from, but the question is: are they reliable?

The first thing you need to do before buying a smoker is:

1. Set your budget:

Make your calculations and state how much you are ready to pay for a smoker. By doing that you will eliminate so many unnecessary options that will waste your time and you will get straight to that smokers that match or are under your price.

2. What is the size of your smoker?

Small smokers tend to cook enough food for up to 20 people so you will always be limited to cook for family only. Big smokers can produce much more then that and are great for big families' reunions as well as parties... You can always check the label on the smoker to see how many people it can smoke the food for.

3. Do you want a grill or a smoker?

You may want to re-think again and see if you want a smoker or a grill? The amazing thing about some smokers is that you can use them in ore then one way. If you don't have a grill and you were consider buying one, this is the perfect opportunity for you to do it because when you get grill-smoker; you will save yourself some bucks, time and space as well.

Now that you made your mind and decided your budget, you may want to take a look at some of the most amazing smokers in the market:

1. Primo 778 Extra-Large Oval Ceramic Charcoal Smoker Grill:

This is a grill and smoker at the same time that proved sturdiness and beauty can be found in one product. It is also perfect for grilling and smoking inside door or outside door as you can always take it with you on trips and camping. It so sturdy and reliable not mention that it is also long lasting. So if you want a grill smoker that last for long, think about this one.

Although it is somewhat expensive because you can get it for 1.269 dollars, it is a high quality and deserves that price.

2. Pitmaker BBQ Safe Smoker:

Another expensive smoker that comes with 1,200 squares inches of smoking space, amazing custom color and 4 racks is an amazing deal for 2,900 dollars. Whether you have a small family or large one, if you have parties often, this is the right smoker for you.

3. Pit Barrel Cooker Package:

On the cheap side, you can get this amazing griller and smoker for only 299 dollars. The most amazing thing about it, is that it is light and you can take it with you wherever you are going without worrying about it taking too much space.

4. Smokehouse Products Big Chief Front Load Smoker:

If the Pit Barrel is not what you looking for, you can always head to a much simpler and cheaper choice which is the electric big chief front load smoker that comes with 5 racks with no assembly requirement for only 100 dollars

Homemade Smoker

Do you want to skip going to stores and deciding on which smoker to buy...which will definitely cause you a headache? You can simply make your own smoker and have some fun while doing it.

Here is an amazing and easy method to make your own smoker that at home.

All you need is:

- 1 Flower Pot
- 4 Large washers
- 1 Single burner
- 1 Masonry drill bit
- 1 Grill thermometer
- 2 Nuts for the screws
- 1 Flower pot drain pan
- 8 Cast iron skillet
- 1 Grill grate
- 3 Flower pot feet
- 1 Fence gate handle
- Long screws
- 1 Sheet Automotive Gasket Material

1. Dismembered the whole burner and bolster the wires through the base channel gap of the window box then lift the burner on the base of the vase with some scrap steel tubing.

2. Utilize the stone work boring tool to penetrate openings in the top for the thermometer and the handle mounts. If you couldn't make the openings sufficiently huge, simply squirm the bit around a little bit.

3. Before you install the equipment, cut out bits of the automotive gasket material to be the same size as the washers, and the framework of your handle that will contact the earthenware. The fundamental thought here is to give some padding in the middle of the metal and the earthenware.

4. Once you get that done, set up everything together by utilizing two washers, of expanding size in the middle of the nut and the earthenware then convey the strengths as much as you could then wedge the thermometer in the opening.

5. Make sure that skillet will fit in the pot then cut its handle off.

6. Bolster the wires for the burner through the base opening, and set your cast iron gifted on top of it with some of your most loved smoking wood. Set in your barbecue mesh, and drop the cover on and you're prepared to go.

Wood Types and Uses

Whether you are using a grill or a smoker, you might want to consider knowing the types of woods you're using because it has a great impact on the flavor of your food more then you think.

If you are using charcoal or wood pellets, you should consider the type of wood you are using and the kind of flavors it will add to your foods. Many people are not aware of it, but they are some types of woods that might end up giving a bitter and unbearable flavor to the food if it wasn't used correctly or with a specific type of foods that goes with it.

Some of these common woods are:

Wood Type	Characteristics	Foods It goes well With
Apple	It has a fruity flavor with slight sweetness to it	Chicken and Pork
Birch	Its scent is not too strong but it has a sweet sent similar to maple	Pork and Poultry
Almond	It has sweet scent and flavor	All types of meats
Maple	It has a sweet flavor and a smoky scent to it	Cheese, Pork, Poultry
Cherry	It has fruity and sweet scent to it	Beef, Pork and Poultry
Pecan	It has a nutty scent and flavor	Poultry, beef, Cheese and Pork

Pear	It has a light smoky flavor with a touch of apple	Pork and Chicken
Plum	It has a slight smoky flavor with a light fruity scent	Fish and Pork
Hickory	It has a sweet scent with bacon flavor	Pork, Ham and Beef
Walnut	It has a very heavy and bitter smoky flavor, it is better to used with another sweet wood	All types of meats
Lilac	It is so light with an amazing floral scent to it	Lamb and Seafood
Orange	It has a mix of citrus and orange scent to it	Fish, poultry, Beef and Pork
Oak	It has a light smoky flavor and scent.	Beef, Wild Fowl, Fish, Poultry and Lamb
Grapev ines	It has a very rich fruity flavor	All types of meat, Poultry

Now that you know all about the types of woods, light up that smoker and get ready to have a nice flavored meal.

Pit and Fire Management

Now that you know all about the basics of buying the right cut of meat and purchasing the right smoker that suits you, it is time for you to jump into the next step which is learning how to pit and manage the fire of your smoker especially if it was a charcoal or wood pellets smoker.

Many of you will start wondering why this chapter is included, almost everybody know how to set up a fire; which is true but the real question is: do you know how to manage the temperature of you smoker and keep it on the right level?

Propane and electric smokers are easy to use and you don't have to keep checking on them to make sure that the temperature didn't change but for the charcoal and wood pellet smokers it quite the opposite. Although they a great smoking method that add more flavor to your food, they comes with a price which is your close attention. Smoking with wood or charcoal can be a difficult task and many people end up with a bad smelling or burnt food because they don't know the basics of using them.

However that will change with these simple tips and tricks that will enable you to get the best out of your wood pellet or charcoal smoker without any single mistake.

For the charcoal smoker, what you need to is:

1. Light the Charcoal:

The first thing that many people do wrong is lighting the coal directly with petroleum, which leaves a bad scent and flavor in the food. The best way to light the coal is by placing a newspaper or a magazine outside of your smoker then pile up the coal on top of it.

Lit the newspaper then leave it lit the coals while it brining. You can then place the coals in your smoker or you can

27

simply avoid all this process and light instead with charcoal lighter.

2. Add some Flavor with Woods:

Using a charcoal smoker doesn't mean that you can't add something else to it; you can always add some soaked chunks of wood of your favorite types of woods to enhance and add more flavor to your food with its smell.

3. Control the Oxygen:

Many people struggle to keep the temperature of their smokers on a set level and when they try to improve it; they end up doing something completely wrong and ruining their whole meal instead.

If you want to control the temperature of your smoker you need to control the oxygen that goes in and comes out of it. The ideal method to do that is by placing a thermometer on the top vet of the grill then checking it from time to time to see if the temperature is lower or higher then you want. If it is low, all you need to do it to open the vent for a while to allow the oxygen to go in and raise it. If it is higher then you want then keep the vent closed and it will be reduced gradually.

4. Adjust the Coal for a Long or Short Period of Time:

If you intend to smoke your food for a short period of time up to 3 or 4 h, all you have to do is to light the entire batch of coal to speed up the process and smoke your food faster. If you want to smoke it for a longer time then all you need to do is to lit up few coals and allow it to burn until it becomes ashes then pour it on top of the other coal. This method will lit the coal slowly and smoke the food for up to 15 h.

28

When it comes to wood pellet smokers there are also easy to use, just fill the hopper with smoking pellets, switch on the smoker then let do what it does best. The only thing that shares with the charcoal smoker is the problem of temperature; in that case you can use the same method by simply opening the vent to raise the temperature or keep it shut to lower it.

The most important thing about using wood pellet smoker is choosing the right wood that will add a nice flavor to your food. You can always check the table above for more information on types of woods and what they go well with.

Now that you know all about managing your smoker and adjusting it temperature, it time to head the most important and fun part which is: Choosing the right cuts of meat to smoke!!!!!!!!

Trimming Meats: The Best Cuts to Smoke

Many people think that the best and most expensive cuts of meats are always perfect for all types of cooking; which is partially true, but what many people don't know is that when it comes to smoking meat, you will have to do things differently.

When it comes to smoking meat; lean, tender and expensive cuts of meats should be the last on your list because they will end up being dry and chewy if you smoked them. The best choice in this case is to use the cheapest and unwanted cuts that are full of fats; it might sound strange but that's what smoking meat is about. It turn the most unwanted cuts that people including you often ignore into the most tender, juicy and flavored ones.

When it comes to pork, lamb, calf or beef; the cheapest cuts are always the start of smokers but that doesn't mean that any cut can be as perfect as the others. There are some specific cuts that are simply perfect for smoking; you can never go wrong with them.

1. The Brisket:

When it comes to smoking meat, the brisket is the king of all cuts; you can never go wrong with it. It is situated in the chest of the cow and people love it because it is so simple and easy to smoke and cook not to mention that it is also tender, full of juices and have a buttery texture that makes it melts in the mouth.

Trimming Tips and Tricks: Before trimming you brisket and deciding whether to remove some fat from it or not, make sure first that fat is more then ¼ inch, because that fat is what will keep your brisket juicy and prevent it from drying. If the fat layer is more the ¼ inch then you can trim it to ¼ inch because too much fat will prevent the brisket from being cooked properly.

2. The Ribs:

Many people think that ribs are not a good cut for smoking because they might become dry but they are absolutely wrong. If you managed to smoke them in the right way they will turn out as good as the brisket. It doesn't matter if you get beef or pork ribs, spare baby back ribs because they are all delicious and will make an amazing smoked meal.

Trimming Tips and Tricks: The first essential step that you need to keep in your mind when you want to trim ribs is to remove the membrane that is situated on the back. Use a sharp and pointy knife to make a small and shallow but then press your finger inside and remove it. From then you can choose if you want to smoke the whole rib as it is or if you want to remove the meat between the bones for a later use.

3. Bacon:

Bacon is an amazing cut that can be used in many ways, thanks to the fat in it stays tender and full juices; which gives it a spot among the best cuts to smoke. You can also make your own bacon at home by simply choosing a nice belly pork cut and then remove its skin and rub it with some salt to protect it from the bacteria then use cold smoking method to smoke it. In a matter of hours, you will have your own homemade smoked bacon that can dry and hot smoke it later...

Trimming Tips: The belly cut comes with a hard skin that prevent the flavors as well as the salt from reaching the meat, so you have to make sure to remove it first carefully by making a small cut with a sharp knife then remove it with your hands the rest of the way.

4. The Pork Butt:

The pork butt is an amazing cut to smoke especially if you have a party and you want to feed lot of people, although it takes lot of time to be cooked properly but it is always a great selection that is so easy to trim. First of all, search for a pork butt that has a red or pink color as well as a layer of fat on top.

The pork butt is already full of fat from the inside so you won't need that layer of fat on the outside, too much fat will make the meat taste "different". Pat dry the pork but then remove the layer of fat on top of the cut without puncturing the meat, which will make the surface of the pork butt crispy and absolutely delicious.

Trimming Tips: If you intend to smoke pork butt and trim it by yourself, make sure to do it with a sharp knife; so you won't end up cutting and damaging the meat in the process or you can simply ask the butcher to do it for you and save yourself a lot of time and effort.

The Cooking: Tips and Tricks

Now that you know all about buying the right smoker and how to handle it as well as how to choose the right cuts to smoke; it is time to master the art of smoking meat. You might think that smoking meat is the easiest part because all you need to do is to heat your smoker and smoke your meat; but have you ever considered improving your way of smoking you meat and learn how you can make it juicier and more delicious?

Maybe you already did but you didn't find any accurate and reliable information on what you are looking for, or you simply never thought about it. Either way, grab a highlighter pen and get ready to know all about the basics and art of smoking meat. Smoking is not the hardest thing to do and not the easiest thing either, all you need to do to master it is to follow some tips and techniques that will be forever embedded in your mind and you will never go wrong when it come smoking any type of meat again.

As a smoker you tend to be somewhat a controller, you like to control and decide everything when it comes to smoking meat. It is not something to be embarrassed about and I bet all smokers have this attitude "even myself" when you want to smoke any type of meat, you want to control everything and you don't like it when someone tells you to add something or remove something because smoking is your special thing that enables you to make something so beautiful and delicious like smoked meat. However, in an attempt to improve your skills in smoking meat and add more flavor to your meat, you might end up following the wrong information that will not add any value to your skills, it will only ruin your meat.

To cut the road short for you and save you from losing your time while trying to look for some information all over the net that might be false, here are some professional tips and techniques for smoking meat that were used several times and proved to be successful in each time.

1. Use the right amount of charcoal/pellet/wood:

Every smoker likes to add his touch to what he is cooking and try to improve it in anyway, and sometime you might end up adding more charcoal or pellets then the manufacturer recommended thinking that it will improve the taste of the meat and cook faster.

That is where you are wrong; smoking is all about cooking meat in a very slow pace and if you are not willing to wait the right period of time for you meat to be cooked properly, then maybe you shouldn't bother smoking your meat in the first place because it will simply end up horrible.

It is great for to you to want improve yourself and skills to make a better job, but you have to check the information you get first before implying them and adding more charcoal or pellets then the manufacturer recommended will result a total fail; because that addition will produce more smoke and flavor which will make your meat look gray and might as well taste somewhat bitter, that is why you need to always stick to the instruction of the manufacturer because they already know the capacity and the best way to use your smoker.

2. Ask for advice from your butcher:

From the beginning of the book I have stated how much befriending the butcher is a necessary step for every smoker and here again another necessary step that require you to befriend your butcher if you want some nice and juicy smoked cuts of meat. If you continue reading this book to the end, you will find some very useful information on how to smoke some specific cuts of meat and the perfect temperature for them, however these information are general and don't have specific information for every cut of meat you will buy, but your butcher definitely does.

So make it a habit to ask you butcher for the best cuts of meat that you can smoke as well as some of information on how you can add more flavor to it and the perfect temperature for it to be cooked. In addition to this valuable information he will give you, this will make a great start for your friendship.

34

3. Pick the wood that will go with the meat your smoking:

If you are using a pellet smoker, make sure to choose the right pellet flavor that goes well with the type of meat you are cooking because it will have a huge impact on it. If the flavor is right, you will get some nice smoked cuts but if it is not, you will end up with bitter meat. There is a whole chapter in this book about the types of woods and what they go well with under the title "Wood Types Uses", you can always use it as a great and reliable reference.

4. More fat means juicy meat:

The fat is the key ingredient to have a juicy and tender cut, so don't even think about getting rid of it because you will end up with tough, dry and chewy meat. If the fat in your cut is too much, you can always trim it but make sure to leave enough of it that will keep your cut of meat moist and melts in the mouth. For more information on trimming your cuts of meat appropriately, check the chapter under the title "Trimming Meat".

5. Prevent your smoked meat from drying out:

If you are one of the smokers that leave the meat in the smoker even when it is done, you should stop doing it. You may have noticed that although you leave lot of fat on the meat cuts they become dry, what you don't know is the act of leaving the meat in the smoker when it is done, is the one the causes it to become dry and chewy; which will make all your efforts go in vain.

Another thing that will cause your meat to lose its juices and dry out is when you slice it or puncture it with a knife to check if it is done. To avoid that, all you have to do is to make a cut in the meat while it is raw before smoking it, so when you want to check if it is done, you can easily place the thermometer in it.

Another mistake that might be doing as well is slicing the meat right after getting out from the smoker. Once the meat is done, remove it from the smoker and rest it as it is from 5 to 15 min before slicing it; otherwise it will lose all its juices and end dry.

Now that you know all about the trips and tricks you need to make some great smoked meat, it time to start on the temperature chart that will give you all the information you need on how long some common cuts of meat should be cooked, the right temperature to cook them with and when you will know that they are done.

Cuts of Meat	Cooking Temperature	Cooking Time	Finish Temperature
Sliced Brisket	225 F/107 C	1.5 H/P	190 F/87 C
Spare Ribs	225 F/107 C	6 to 7 H/P	Tender
Pulled Pork Butt	225 F/107 C	1.5 H	205 F/96 C
Beef Ribs	225 F/107 C	3 to 4 H	175 F/79 C
Chopped Brisket	225 F/107 C	1.5 H/p	200 F/93 C
Baby Back Ribs	225 F/107 C	5 to 6 H	Tender

How to keep you meat moist and full of flavors:

Rubbing and marinating the cuts of meats doesn't require any skills or certain techniques, the choice is always yours to choose a certain spices rub or marinate whether you made it home or bought it from stores or you can simply use some salt and pepper and be surprised how much your meat will be delicious.

Before rubbing or marinating a meat cut, make sure to pat dry it first gently with some paper towel, don't be too rough with it and press it hard because you will remove all the moisture from it and end up with a dry cut of meat. All you need to do is pat it gently then rub it with your selection of spices or marinate, you can marinate it for 4 to 5 h but it is highly recommended to leave it for an overnight; that way it will absorb the flavors and become more delicious.

Another easy way to make the cut of meat maintain its juices is to wrap it in a paper foil, that way all the juices that comes out of the meat will not go to waste and will be preserved instead in the paper foil. If you want to add more flavor to your cut of meat, poor up to ¼ cup of apple juice or chicken broth...in the paper foil then place in it the meat cut and seal it; this will enable the meat to absorb more flavor and juice which will make it moist and tender.

If you don't like both ways and prefer to cook your meat without wrapping it, you can simply fill a pan with water if you don't have one in your smoker then place it on top of the charcoal or pellets in the fire chamber. This method will keep the meat tender and moisturized without affecting its taste or flavor, you may have heard some people suggests replacing the water with beer, apple juice or wine; don't even think about it. If you replaced the water with another liquid, it will change the taste and flavor of the meat and you might end up with a smelly meat with a bad taste.

Serving and Eating

Congratulations, you just passed a long road and learned the basics of smoking meats that will leave the people you cook for surprised with your skills and asking for tips on how to become a great smoker like you.

You know now how to buy nice cuts of meats with a reasonable price, you learned the characteristics of all types of smokers and how you can work with them and you learnt how to build a smoker from scratch.

You know now the types of woods used for smoking and which type of meats they will go well with, you learned how to light up your charcoal or pellet smoker and how to maintain the same temperature, you learned how to trim meats and prepare them for the smoker.

You know now the temperature that you should cook certain cuts of meat in, for how long to cook them and when they are done and you learned the best techniques and tricks to keep the cuts of meats moist, juicy and tender.

However the basics of meat are not completed without appropriately serving your perfectly smoked cuts of meat and share them with your family.

One of the most important steps of serving smoked cuts of meats is slicing it. You may have noticed that when you smoke a cut of meat it turns out amazingly juicy and tender but once you sliced it loses almost all it juice and become chewy and dry. That's why you need to learn the basics of slicing because it is your fault the meat loses its juice.

Once you decide to smoke a brisket, a pork butt or anything that requires slicing when it is smoked, you have to purchase a nice sharp knife that doesn't have any pointy teethes, because it will make the slicing process smooth and prevent your cuts of meat from losing its juices.

Grab the cut of meat gently without pressing it then slice it in half, then grab each half gently and slice it into ¼ inch slices.

The Best Sauces and Side Dishes to Serve with Smoked Meat

Smoked meat is known to be full of fats, so the best sides to serve it with needs to be fresh and low in fat to balance your meal as well as some beer to help you digest all those fats.

Here are some simple light salads and sauces that will make a wonderful meal with your smoked meat:

Spicy and Sweet Marinate

Serves: 4

Prep Time: 5 min

Ingredients:

- 1 cup of honey
- 4 cups of ketchup
- ½ cup of Worcestershire sauce
- 1 ½ cup of brown sugar
- ½ cup of apple cider vinegar
- 1 tablespoon of onion powder
- 1 tablespoon of garlic powder
- 2 cups of jalapeno peppers, seeded
- Black pepper
- Salt

Directions:

1. Combine all the ingredients in food processer then blend them smooth.

2. Marinate the beef, lamb or pork with the sauce then chill it in the fridge for 4 to an overnight then smoke it and enjoy.

Soda Sauce

Serves: 4 to 8

Prep Time: 5 min

Ingredients:

- 1 cup of ketchup
- ¼ cup of chili sauce
- 2 cups of doctor pepper soda
- 3 tablespoons of apple cider vinegar
- 2 tablespoons of Worcestershire sauce
- 2 teaspoons of garlic, finely chopped

Directions:

1. Combine all the ingredients in a food processer and blend them smooth.

2. Pour the sauce in a saucepan then bring it to a boil.

3. Lower the heat and simmer it for 20 to 30 min until it thickness slightly then serve it with smoked meat or chicken and enjoy.

Tomato Chips

Serves: 4 to 8

Prep Time: 10 min

Ingredients:

- 1 pound (454 g) of green tomato, sliced
- ½ cup of canola oil
- ½ cup of purpose flour
- 3 eggs, beaten
- ½ cup of yellow corn meal
- Black pepper
- Salt

Directions:

1. Preheat the canola oil in a skillet.

2. Season the slices of tomato with some salt and black pepper then dip in the purpose flour followed by the beaten eggs and corn meal.

3. Deep fry the tomato until it becomes golden and crispy then serve it and enjoy.

Mango Salad

Serves: 6

Prep Time: 1 h

Ingredients:

- 1 cup of mango, diced
- 2 tablespoons of lemon juice
- 1 small red onion, sliced
- 1 cucumber, seedless and diced
- ¼ cup of cilantro, finely chopped
- 2 teaspoons of olive oil
- Black pepper
- Salt

Directions:

1. Combine all the ingredients in a serving bowl then toss them gently.

2. Chill the salad in the fridge for 30 to 45 min then serve it and enjoy.

Fruits Salad

Serves: 4 to 8

Prep Time: 10 min

Ingredients:

- 4 cups of strawberries, halved
- 2 cups of mango, diced
- 1 cup of pineapple, diced
- ¼ cup of lime juice
- ¼ cup of sugar
- 2 cups of melon, diced
- Black pepper
- Salt

Directions:

1. Combine the sugar with lemon juice and stir it to dissolve.

2. Combine all the ingredients in a large serving bowl then stir them gently.

3. Chill the salad in the fridge for 15 to 20 min then serve it and enjoy.

The Top 25 Smoked Meat, Sauces, Rubs Recipes

I hope you enjoyed these 25 delicious "Smoked Meat" recipes, and I hope you share them with your family and friends.

Chili Sweet Rub
(ready in about 5 min | Servings 2 1/3 cup)

Ingredients:

- 2 tablespoons of chili pepper
- 2 tablespoons of garlic powder
- 2 tablespoons of cayenne pepper
- ½ cup of paprika
- 1 cup of sugar
- 2 tablespoons of lemon pepper
- 2 tablespoons of kosher salt
- 2 tablespoons of onion powder
- 2 tablespoons of black pepper

Directions:

1. Combine all the ingredients in a small bowl and mix them.
2. Transfer the rub into a storage container or use it right away.

Multi-purpose Rub

(ready in about 5 min | Servings 1/3 cup)

Ingredients:

- 1 tablespoons of Chinese five spices powder
- 2 teaspoons of ginger powder
- ¼ teaspoon of cayenne pepper
- 1 teaspoon of kosher salt
- 1 teaspoon of onion powder
- 1 teaspoon of garlic powder
- 2 tablespoons of brown sugar

Directions:

1. Mix all the ingredients in a small bowl until they become smooth.
2. Use your rub right away or store it in a storage container.

Basic Rub
(ready in about 5 min | Servings 1/3 cup)

Ingredients:

- 2 tablespoons of garlic powder
- 2 tablespoon of kosher salt
- 2 tablespoon of black pepper

Directions:

1. Mix all the ingredients in a small bowl then use them right away or store them in a container.

Honey Sauce
(ready in about 5 min | Servings 4 cups)

Ingredients:

- ½ cup of ketchup
- ¼ cup of light brown sugar
- ½ cup of butter
- 1 cup of honey
- 1 cup of Dave's sweet and zesty barbeque sauce
- ¼ cup of orange juice
- 2 tablespoons of white sugar
- 3 tablespoons of Dijon mustard
- 1 tablespoon of garlic powder
- 1 tablespoon of chili powder
- 2 tablespoons of black pepper

- 2 tablespoons of soy sauce
- 2 tablespoons of white vinegar

Directions:

1. Combine all the ingredients in a saucepan then simmer them for 15 min on low heat.
2. Once the time is up, use it right away or store it in a storage container.

Spicy Black Sauce
(ready in about 5 min | Servings 1 cup)

Ingredients:

- ¼ cup of honey
- ¾ cup of hoisin sauce
- 1 teaspoon of sriracha sauce

Directions:

1. Whisk all the ingredients in a small bowl until they become smooth.
2. Use your sauce right away or store it in a storage container.

Garlicky Mashed Potato
(ready in about 1 h | Servings 6)

Ingredients:

- 1/3 cup of heavy cream
- 2 ½ pounds of potatoes, peeled and quartered
- 1 bulb of garlic
- ¼ cup of butter
- ½ teaspoon of black pepper
- ½ teaspoon of salt

Directions:

1. Heat the oven on 360 F.
2. Slice the top of the garlic bulb and brush it with some vegetable oil then wrap it in a piece of foil and broil it for 5 min.
3. Place the potato in a stockpot and cover it with water and a pinch of salt then bring it to a boil.
4. Lower the heat and simmer the potatoes for 20 to 30 min or until it soften.

5. Once the time is up, drain the potato and place it in a bowl then add squeeze into it right away the garlic with butter and a pinch of black pepper.
6. Mash the potato with a fork until it becomes smooth and the butter melts then add to it the cream gradually while mashing it.
7. Serve it warm and enjoy.

Smoked Salmon Spread
(ready in about 5 min | Servings 2 cups)

Ingredients:

- 3 tablespoons of lemon juice
- 1 cup of smoked salmon fillet, flakes
- 1 teaspoon of cumin
- ¼ cup of fresh chives, finely chopped
- 8 ounces of cream cheese, softened

Directions:

1. Combine all the ingredients in a small serving bowl and stir them gently then serve it and enjoy.

Spicy Coleslaw Salad
(ready in about 10 min | Servings 8)

Ingredients:

- 2 tablespoons of heavy cream
- 1 cup of carrots, shredded
- 1 small onion, grated
- 2 jalapenos, minced
- 2 tablespoons of cumin
- 4 cups of green, shredded
- ½ cup of red cabbage, shredded
- ½ cup of mayonnaise
- 1 teaspoon of sugar 1 teaspoon of lemon juice
- ¼ teaspoon of salt
- ½ teaspoon of Tabasco sauce

Directions:

1. Combine all the carrots with green and red cabbage, jalapeno and onion in a serving bowl and set it aside.
2. Combine the rest of the ingredients in a small bowl and whisk them until they become smooth.
3. Pour the sauce all over the veggies and toss it gently then serve it and enjoy.

55

Summer Salad
(ready in about 10 min | Servings 3 ½ cups)

Ingredients:

- 2 small jalapeno pepper, seeded and chopped
- 2 cups of tomato, diced
- 1 small onion, finely chopped
- 1 small clove of garlic, minced
- ¼ to ½ cup of parsley leaves, finely chopped
- 1 tablespoon of lemon juice
- ¼ teaspoon of salt

Directions:

1. Combine all the ingredients in a bowl and toss them gently then serve them and enjoy.

Cheese Sticks

(ready in about 1 h | Servings 24)

Ingredients:

- 24 cheese sticks

Directions:

1. Prepare the smoker for cold smoking.
2. Lay the cheese sticks in the smoker then apply light smoke for 1 h on 90 F.
3. Once the time is up, place the sticks directly in a zip lock and refrigerate them for 10 days before using them.

Smoked Corn on the Cob
(ready in about 2 h 15 min| Servings 6 to 8)

Ingredients:

- 6 to 8 ears of corn kernels on cobs
- 1 teaspoon of kosher salt
- 1 teaspoon of black pepper
- ½ cup of butter, softened
- ¼ cup of olive oil

Directions:

1. Pull the husks down without removing them completely then remove all the silk from it.
2. Mix the olive oil with pepper and salt in a small bowl then rub the corncobs with it and pull the husks back to place.
3. Preheat the smoker on 240 F then smoke them for 30 min.
4. Rub some of the butter all over the cobs and smoke them for 1 h 30 min while rubbing them with butter every 30 min.

5. Once the time is up, serve them warm and enjoy.

Cheesy Smoked Pork's Shepherd Pie
(ready in about 30 min | Servings 6 to 8)

Ingredients:

- 2 cups of cheddar cheese, shredded
- 2 cups of pepper jack cheese, shredded
- 8 cups of "Garlicky Potato Mash"
- 4 cups of "Smoked Pork Butt"

Directions:

1. Pour 4 cups of garlicky potato mash in the bottom of a greased baking dish followed by the pulled pork, pepper jack cheese, cheddar cheese and another layer of potato.
2. Preheat the oven on 350 F and bake the pie for 20 min then serve it warm and enjoy.

Coleslaw Barbecue
(ready in about 5 h | Servings 4)

Ingredients:

- 1 recipe of "Smoked Pork Butt"
- 1 recipes of "Spicy Coleslaw Salad"

Directions:

1. Assemble your burgers using the pulled pork with coleslaw salad and enjoy.

Smoked Fajitas
(ready in about 20 min| Servings 5)

Ingredients:

- 1 smoked brisket in a pan
- 2 red and yellow bell peppers, julienned
- 4 cups of pulled "brisket pan"
- 10 (8 inches) flour tortillas
- 1 jalapeno pepper, sliced
- 5 tablespoons of vegetable oil
- 2 cups of "summer salad"
- 2 cups of cheddar cheese, shredded
- 1 cup of sour cream
- 1 red onion, sliced

Directions:

1. Heat 3 tablespoons of vegetable oil in a skillet then sauté in the onion with pepper and jalapeno for 5 to 7 min until they soften.

2. In the mean time, heat the rest of the oil in a frying pan and fry in it the tortillas until they become brown from both sides.
3. Assemble your sandwiches the way you like it then serve them and enjoy.

Smokey Apple Pie
(ready in about 3 h | Servings 4)

Ingredients:

- 4 (9 inches) frozen piecrusts, thawed
- 4 apples, cored and diced
- 1 1/3 cup of brown sugar
- 1 cup of butter, melted
- ¼ cup of milk
- 4 teaspoons of lemon juice
- 1 teaspoon of cinnamon

Directions:

1. Knead 1 piecrust to a boil then divide it into in half and roll them until they become ¼ inch thick.

2. Line up the bottom of 4 inches greased ramekins with one of the dough halves then cut the rest of it into stripes or circles.
3. Mix the lemon juice with apple in a small bowl and set it aside.
4. Combine the brown sugar cinnamon and butter in a bowl and mix them then stir in the apples.
5. Spoon the mix into the 4 ramekins and cover them with circles or stripes of the dough.
6. Preheat the smoker on 375 F for 30 min.
7. Place the ramekin directly on the grate and smoke them until the apples soften using a toothpick to check them.
8. Once the time is up, allow them to cool down completely then serve them and enjoy.

Perfectly Smoked Cornish Game Hens
(ready in about 5 h | Servings 4 to 8)

Ingredients:

- 4 Cornish Game Hens
- ½ cup of butter
- 2 tablespoons of "basic rub"

Directions:

1. Rinse the hens and pat them dry then sprinkle each hen with ½ tablespoon of the rub.
2. Set the hens aside to 45 min and heat the smoker on 240 F.
3. Place the hens in the smoker with their breasts facing down and smoke them for 4 h.
4. Melt the butter then baste the hens every 45 min to keep them moist.
5. Once the time is up, wrap them with foil for 15 min then serve them and enjoy.

Rubbed and Smoked Chicken
(ready in about 3 to 4 h | Servings 8)

Ingredients:

Rub:

- ¼ cup of yellow mustard
- 1/3 cup of "basic rub"

- 2 (4 pounds) whole chickens

Directions:

1. Mix the rub mix in a small bowl then spread 1 tablespoon of it under the skin of each chicken gently without tearing it.
2. Rub the rest of the rub on both chickens.
3. Preheat the smoker on 240 F then place in it the chickens with their breasts facing down and cover their wings with foil.
4. Smoke them for 1 h then flip them and cook them for another 2 h.
5. Once the time is up, allow them to rest for 10 before serving.

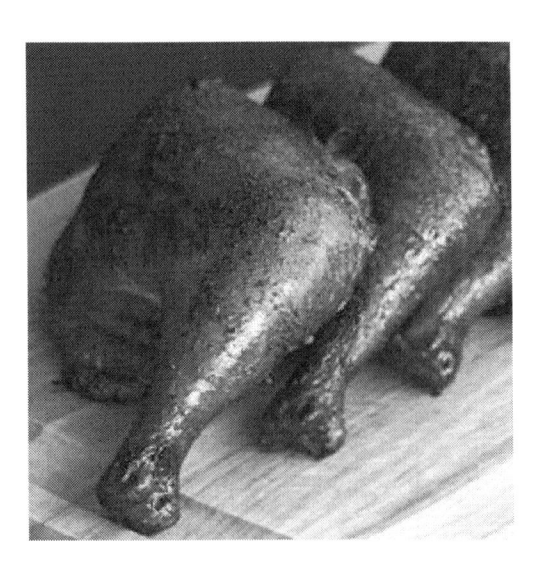

Smoked Quarters
(ready in about 5 h | Servings 6)

Ingredients:

Rub:

- 1/3 cup of "basic rub"
- 2 tablespoons of yellow mustard

- 6 chicken quarters

Directions:

1. Combine the rub ingredients in a small bowl and mix them then apply it to the chicken while trying to get it under the skin without tearing it.
2. Allow the chicken to absorb the flavors for 30 to 45 min the heat the smoker on 240 F.

3. Place the chicken quarters away from each other with 1 inch then smoke them for 4 h.

Smoked Turkey
(ready in about 6 h 45| Servings 10 to 12)

Ingredients:

Rub:

- ½ cup of "basic rub"

- 12 pounds whole turkey

Directions:

1. Apply the rub to the whole turkey and try to get some of the rub under its skin without tearing it.
2. Preheat the smoker on 240 F then place it in the turkey with its breast facing down.
3. Smoke it for 1 h then flip it and smoke it for 5 h 30 min.
4. Once the time is up, allow it to rest for 30 min before serving it and enjoy.

Basic Quarters
(ready in about 11 h 45 | Servings 6 to 8)

Ingredients:

Marinade:

- 6 tablespoons of parsley leaves, finely chopped
- 2 tablespoons of fresh cilantro, finely chopped
- 2 tablespoons of basil, finely chopped
- 2 tablespoons of fresh oregano, finely chopped
- 1 cup of olive oil
- ½ cup of fresh lemon juice
- 1 tablespoon of garlic, minced
- 1 ¾ teaspoons of kosher salt
- ¾ teaspoon of cayenne pepper

- 6 chicken quarters

Directions:

1. Build fire in one side of the smoker leaving the other side empty.
2. Mix all the ingredients of the marinade in a small bowl then reserve ½ cup of it.
3. Combine the rest of the marinade with the chicken in a big resalable bag and refrigerate it for 10 h.
4. Preheat the smoker on 300 F then place the chicken quarters on the empty side and smoke them for 45 min.
5. Once the time is up, flip them and baste them with the rest of the marinade then cook them for another 45 min and serve them warm.

Semi Sweet Smoked Salmon
(ready in about 5 h | Servings 4 to 6)

Ingredients:

Marinade:
- 4 cloves of garlic, crushed
- 1 gallon (16 cups) of water
- ¾ cup of brown sugar
- 1 cup of kosher salt

- 4 pounds of salmon fillets.

Directions:

1. Pour the water in a large container then stir into it the salt until it dissolves followed by the sugar.
2. Place the salmon fillets in a large container then pour on them the marinade with cloves of garlic.
3. Refrigerate the salmon fillets for 2 h to absorb the flavors then drain it from the marinade, rinse it and pat it dry.

4. Preheat the smoker on 1600 F and place the salmon on a parchment paper and smoke it for 4 to 5 h until it reaches 145 F.
5. Serve it warm and enjoy.

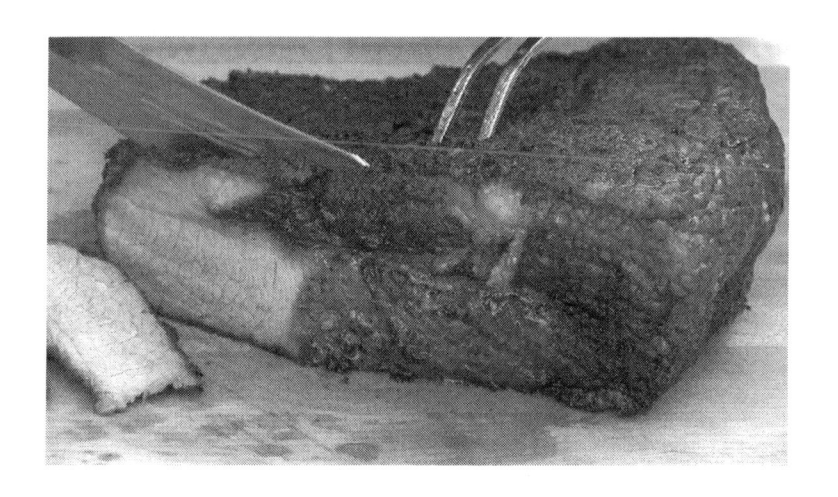

Brisket pan
(ready in about 14 h | Servings 8)

Ingredients:

Rub:

- 2 tablespoons of garlic powder
- 2 tablespoons of black pepper
- 2 tablespoons of kosher salt
- 2 teaspoons of cayenne pepper

- 7 to 9 pounds brisket

Directions:

1. Mix the dry ingredients in a bowl then apply them to the brisket and set it aside for 45 min.
2. Preheat the smoker on 240 F.
3. Place the brisket in a disposable aluminum pan then smoke it for 4 h.

4. Once times it up, cook it for another 4 h while flipping it every 2 h.
5. Once its internal temperature reaches 160 F, cover it with a piece of foil and cook it until it reaches 190 F.
6. Remover the brisket from the smoker and keep basting it with its drippings.

Apple Ribs
(ready in about 6 h | Servings 6)

Ingredients:

Rub:

- ½ cup of apple juice
- ¼ cup of yellow mustard
- 1/3 cup of "basic rub"

- 2 rack of pork spare ribs (4 pounds)

Directions:

1. Heat the smoker 240 F.
2. Massage the 2 racks with mustard followed by the rub then set aside for 30 min.
3. Once the time is up, place them in the smoker and cook them for 3 h.
4. Remove the racks from the smoker and place each on a piece of foil.

5. Pour ¼ cup of apple juice on the ribs and quickly wrap the foil around them then smoke them for another hour.
6. Once the time is up, slice them and serve them.

Smoky Pork Butt

(ready in about 13 h | Servings 6 to 8)

Ingredients:

Rub:

- 1 recipe of "Smoked Pork Butt"
- 1 recipes of "Spicy Coleslaw Salad"

- 7 to 9 pork butt

Directions:

1. Mix the rub with mustard in a small bowl then apply it by massaging it to the pork butt and leave it on the counter for 45 min.
2. Preheat the smoker on 240 F.

3. Place the pork butt on the grate directly then place under an aluminum pan to collect its drippings.
4. Cook for 4 h then insert in it a thermometer and smoke it until its inner temperature becomes 205 F.
5. Once time is up, allow it to rest for 30 min then pull it with a fork.

Dripping Ribs
(ready in about 6 h 15 min| Servings 6)

Ingredients:

Rub:

- 1/3 cup of "multi-purpose" rub
- 1 cup of "Spicy black sauce"
- 3 tablespoons of soy sauce
- 1 cup of apple juice

- 2 racks of pork spare ribs, 4 pounds for each

Directions:

1. Brush the rack of ribs with soy sauce then rub them with the chili rub.
2. Heat the smoker on 240 F then smoke them for 3 h while Spritzing them every once in a while with some apple juice.
3. Once the time is up place the racks in 2 separate pieces of foil and pour on them the rest of the apple juice.

4. Wrap the foil around the racks trapping the juice inside and smoke them for another 2 h.
5. Once the time is up, remove the foil and smoke them for another hour.
6. While brushing them with the spicy black sauce every 30 min.
7. Allow the ribs to rest for 10 to 15 min then serve them and enjoy.

Your Free Gift

I wanted to show my appreciation that you support my work so I've put together a free gift for you.

Slowcooker Essentials Cookbook
http://thezenfactory.com/smoke_like_pro_book/

Just visit the link above to download it now.

I know you will love this gift.

Thanks!

Conclusion

Thank you again for downloading this book! I really do hope you found the recipes as tasty and mouth watering as I did.

☐ **Copyright by Daniel Hinkle- All rights reserved.**

This document is geared towards providing exact and reliable information in regards to the topic and issue covered. The publication is sold with the idea that the publisher is not required to render accounting, officially permitted, or otherwise, qualified services. If advice is necessary, legal or professional, a practiced individual in the profession should be ordered.

- From a Declaration of Principles which was accepted and approved equally by a Committee of the American Bar Association and a Committee of Publishers and Associations.

In no way is it legal to reproduce, duplicate, or transmit any part of this document in either electronic means or in printed format. Recording of this publication is strictly prohibited and any storage of this document is not allowed unless with written permission from the publisher. All rights reserved.

The information provided herein is stated to be truthful and consistent, in that any liability, in terms of inattention or otherwise, by any usage or abuse of any policies, processes, or directions contained within is the solitary and utter responsibility of the recipient reader. Under no circumstances will any legal responsibility or blame be held against the publisher for any reparation, damages, or monetary loss due to the information herein, either directly or indirectly.

Respective authors own all copyrights not held by the publisher.

The information herein is offered for informational purposes solely, and is universal as so. The presentation of the information is without contract or any type of guarantee assurance.

The trademarks that are used are without any consent, and the publication of the trademark is without permission or backing by the trademark owner. All trademarks and brands within this book are for clarifying purposes only and are the owned by the owners themselves, not affiliated with this document.

46384821R00050

Made in the USA
Middletown, DE
30 July 2017